MW00775262

Inheritance: Poems.

Front cover photograph, "Birth of Identity," by David G. Moore.
Used by permission (www.davidgmoore.com).

Front cover concept by Tommy Gear and Jenny Walters.

Back cover photograph by Jenny Walters. Used by permission.

Cover design by Mona Z. Kraculdy.

Some poems previously appeared in: *Best Gay Poetry 2008*, *Eyes of Desire*, *In Other Words*, *The Most Intriguing and Sensual Male Poet Calendar 2006*, *Mirage #4/Period(ical) #135*, *Radical Faerie Digest*, *Sun Scripts*, and *Velvet Mafia*.

Sibling Rivalry Press, LLC
13913 Magnolia Glen Drive
Alexander, AR 72002

www.siblingrivalrypress.com

Library of Congress Control Number: 2011924541

ISBN: 978-0-9832931-2-5

First Sibling Rivalry Press Edition, April 2011

Inheritance

poems

Steven Reigns

Acknowledgments

Much gratitude to Tim Miller, Troy Shields, Jenny Walters, and Eloise Klein Healy for their support in helping shape this book.

Special thanks to: Juliette Aiyana, Noel Alumit, Irvin Lin & AJ Bates, Steve Berman, Bryan Borland, Thaddeus Root & Desmond Clark, Wanda Coleman, Joanne Carrubba & Mike Coulson, Caleb Colravy, Michael Coulombe, Nancy Comeau, the compound guys, Walter DeMilly, Mark Doty, Kim & Josh Dupuis, Alex Epps, Tommy Gear, Amy Gerstler, Jim Gladstone, Hilary Goldberg, Moira Griffin, Kim Hanna, Shannon Headley, Jeff Sullivan & Alan Holt, David Johnson, Michael Kearns, Collin Kelley, Michael Kelley, Swati Khurana, Dodie Bellamy & Kevin Killian, Darin Klein, Scott Kluksdahl, Jessica Leach, Dan Lopez, Ian MacKinnon, Jennifer Mensch, Sean Meriwether, BJ Milan, Betty Moss, Eileen Myles, Sharon Olds and fellow poets at The Key West Literary Workshop & Palm Beach Poetry Workshop, Felice Picano, Renee Rallo, Stephanie Recht, Ariana Watson & Jennifer Roberts, Martha Roper, Corey Roskin, Brian Rush, Jasper Sage, Sapphire and fellow artists at The Atlantic Center for the Arts, Lawrence Schimel, Rob Scott, Jen Smat, Jill Stansbury, Shirley Taylor, John Walsh, Patricia Walters, Edmund White, Chuck Williams, George Williams, John Morgan Wilson, and Lee Wind.

It doesn't matter who my father was;
it matters who I remember he was.

—Anne Sexton

I would not trade this me for a
different childhood, a different mother.

—Robyn Posen

Contents

Dedicated to
My Sister Cindy
and My Family of Friends

SEIZED AND POSSESSED

Dad's Empire

He rubbed my mother's swollen belly.
Dreamt of the All-American Boy he'd raise,
games of catch, putting worms on hooks,
and giving advice on the ladies.
He took photos at the birth.
The second child a boy,
his dreams finally fulfilled.
The family is now complete.
They are the American dream;
suburban home, 2 cars, privacy fence, a dog,
one boy, one girl, a 401k, and secrets we kept.

Out of Gas

The Buick's faulty gas gauge
strands us on I-270.
Tears streaming down the faces
of the stranded
we walk up the embankment.
My 10-year-old sister, myself at 8, and my mother
who soon jumps into the role
she always should have been in:
mother.
She comforts us with words
"It's no big deal."
We reach the top, walk down the long road to civilization.
A car stops and a woman I don't recognize
calls my mother's name.
We are soon in her station wagon
with her flip-flop clad children headed to the pool.
The women chat.
I sit red-eyed and wet-faced looking at the floor,
embarrassed to have been stranded,
to need to be rescued, and
to have been crying.

She asks
"How is your husband with these things?
Would it be best if we just filled the car?"

Two women
with two kids each
trading careers for motherhood
exchanging autonomy for wifely expectations

My mother tells her my father would be fine.
We are dropped off at our house to my father's screams.
The woman was out of the driveway and down the street
before my mother whispered "please don't."

Crouched in the corner
I daydream about the children in the pool—
cannonballs
belly flops
Marco Polo
and leaking goggles.

Playing with the Doll

He'd undress her, slipping overalls off her stiff shoulders,
push them down to the cement basement floor.
Her four-foot plastic body stood
as if she were a frigid woman
not wanting to be touched, stone-still in fear.
He'd throw the naked doll down face first,
press his thick body against
the jaundiced glow of her synthetic skin.
He'd writhe on top of her,
a young boy of nine grinding his hips
into the part of her legs, where if she were flesh, there would be a hole.
I sat in the corner and watched
as the real humped the unreal.
I let it all happen out of relief that I was not her,
that my clothes were still on,
that his body was not pressed against me.

When it was me, I was as motionless as she
as silent as she.

While he ground into her plastic body
I wondered who he liked more.
This is when I thought touch was love,
this is when I thought what he did to me was a sign of love.

His rifling and raping of the doll did not elicit fear or desire,
just wonder at how all of this felt to him.
I wondered about the overweight boy with harsh cold hands
who would hold me down, touch me, and
find a replacement for me in this doll.

He finished and we went upstairs.
Later my mother would find her;

matted blond hair, naked, face first on the ground,
a violated synthetic woman.
She would ask me, in my youthful honesty I would tell her
it was him, it was the neighbor
who frottaged and fucked the oversized Patty Play Pal.

"You're such a liar, don't blame it on anyone else.
You're sick Steven."
It didn't really bother me not to be believed.
Like my father's fist, my mother's backhand,
my neighbor's weight on me
it was commonplace
and I was the stone-faced doll that took it.

Rifle

The cold steel touches my cheek.
I squint,
an attempt at securing accurate vision.

My finger doesn't itch
or pull.
It is more like a spasm.
Shock waves stun my shoulder
as hundreds of pellets hurl at the target.

This is the sport my father taught me,
this was the area he wanted me to excel in.
He wanted me to kill.

I regain my balance.
My shoulder will bruise a lighter shade
than the purple welts that covered my body in boyhood.
I check the target.
I am a good shot,
a sign of my father's influence
and a sign of years of practice to become
the boy my daddy wanted.

I excelled in his arena
And, yes Dad,
I want to kill.

Cocking the rifle
I squint—a faggot with good aim—
and keep firing.

After the Ballgame

I'm on the toilet,
pants around my ankles.

My mother knocks,
opens the door,
lets herself in
to the bathroom
after a baseball game
I was forced to play.
I should have locked the door.

I'm naked,
exposed, vulnerable.
I am captive.

She sits on the edge of the bathtub
and talks to me about
how much I embarrass her—my light voice,
my limp wrists,
my lack of baseball ability.

"You know, if you keep acting like a girl
maybe we should start putting you in dresses."

I cannot think of ways to leave this situation.
My pants and underwear rest on my cleats.
My ass dirty,

my torso naked,
"You seem to want to be a girl.
Maybe we could go to the doctor and he can make you a girl."

I sit humiliated listening to her words of degradation.

Teased in the halls of school,
spit wads aimed at me on the bus
and now this.

The toilet, the timing, the topic
keeps me from retelling the story for twenty years.
Still blaming myself
for being girly and not locking the door.

She will not mention this conversation again.
I don't either, out of fear of hearing her words.
This is when I thought
silence would protect me.

Bottle Tosser

Cranking down the window
techno blaring
car speeding at and above the limit,
I hurl the bottle onto the embankment,
my notoriety
riding shotgun
with a good arm.
Not only was I hanging out with people
my mother warned me about,
I was one of them.
Not only an open container contender and consumer,
I littered to escape the law.

Bottles from the backseat were passed to me
as the inebriated passengers marveled at the throw
by the fag who spent years in right field,
coerced to play catch for parental aims
of becoming a baseball star.

Caps, cleats, and cups were to make me what they wanted,
not what they feared.
It didn't make me less gay,
it just gave me a stronger arm.

Stolen

I was startled to see him there.
He was equally startled,
for a different reason.
He was stealing from me.
My car window smashed, door opened, and trunk ajar.
I looked from his round face to the mini-van
filled with thug friends and my car's possessions.
I shouted to "get out" before he took his first step.
Waved my fist in the air, like someone
who was accustomed to using it.
He hopped into the mini-van and rode off.

It is an odd experience to see robbers,
kids the age of the children I had taught.
But these kids were different,
they were stealing.
The police report stated the lost items:
15 copies of the same book,
a toolbox filled with pottery tools,
a 25 lb bag of clay,
CDs,
a blanket.

Of course, I wish for my possessions back.
A part of me wants them to keep them and use them.
I imagine
stoned, high, or drunk, one of the young men
pulls clay from the bag
rolls it on the table that drug deals are made on,
starts coiling a mug or bowl.

He pulls my tools out of the box, shapes his masterpiece.
The drug and my well-worn tools in his hand

make him feel like an artist, like someone
who has talent—not a thief.

And what of the books?
The boy I saw in the passenger seat will pick one up,
read it cover to cover. Cry over all that he has lost,
all that has been stolen from him,
over the neighbor he couldn't stop,
over the father he didn't know.
Maybe the man who had his fist in the air becomes more human,
so human guilt that he stifles surfaces
with the drug that led him to stealing.

Maybe I screamed too early.
I should have asked what he was looking for,
told him what he wants
is not in my car, my house, my neighborhood.
It is inside him. I do not know his life, his story, or his name
but I know I saw a young man worthy of love.
His breath alone gives him that right
and his actions keep us from seeing it.

Losing Things

Babe, Where are my grey slacks?
Hon, have you seen my keys?
Beautiful, where is the checkbook?

My father was always losing things.
He'd preface his question with a flattering nicety to my mother.
My mother was the net, catching everything he lost.
He never seemed to be able to hold onto things,
including his temper.

That's foolish
Why are you doing such a thing?
You ignoramus
Don't be stupid
Give it to me, I'll do it.

In my case, the niceties were left out.

My Mother Applies for a Job

She sat at the kitchen table and
labored over the grammar and spelling of her thank you notes.

They said they would call her on Monday.
She waited day and night
near the anticipated
ringing phone.

She wanted it badly.

A woman with plenty of experience for the position
and no esteem to believe it could really be hers.
She didn't leave the house,
she wasn't going to until they called.
I reminded her of the answering machine.
She cried,
told me of another woman
whom they also interviewed.
"If I'm not home they might call her."
My mother,
a woman who believed she was that easily replaceable
and stayed indoors for a week
waiting for a call.

Legal Pads

I met him online,
pressed in an e-mail for his number.
His confession followed.
Even if I had his number to dial,
he wouldn't be able to hear me
on the other end.

We soon found ways of contact
and would sit on my couch
having conversations
on legal pads.

It was on that lined paper I was told
of his Midwest childhood,
Gallaudet University,
rude waiters,
and the maddening base driven music at gay clubs.

After 3 dates and 4 filled notepads,
the hands with which he spoke to others explored my body.
Speaking with touch, not the pen,
tracing details I had long forgotten:
the circular scar on my shin,
the folds of my ear, and
my ticklish belly.
Through out it all I heard his sounds—
the deep primal uttering of excitement or fascination.

We'd see foreign films at a rundown theatre.
The poor sound system inconsequential
as we read each yellowed word at the screen's edge.
I became accustomed to a shaking bed waking me up,

a flickering light signifying company,
and no radio in the car.

He and I, out of necessity, scribed our desires
Each scrawled sentence purposeful and precise.

When he was not with me, I'd reread our legal pads.
Each line sealing my memory of that moment.
I reread the lines of his love for me,
something to reference later.
That his feeling was documented
felt more authentic, unshakeable,
almost unrefuted
like a legal document itself.

Cocaine

In that white powder
I found the esteem I always lacked.
Found the results of morning affirmations,
found happiness as it drained down the back of my throat.

My body an alchemy machine
that turned a drug into self-acceptance.

I hated key bumps.
They were never enough.
I'd do the thick straight lines called rails.

And while coke worked its wonder
I could dance, fuck,
maybe conquer the world.

My parents loved with limits,
but with my rolled bill and razor
my love knew no limits,
no bounds.

The drug guided me to the inheritance
my parents deprived me of—unconditional love.

I was a cocaine cowboy
exploring the uncharted terrain
of self-love.

Two Atlases

We both set down our worlds.
Our hands find homes.
Our lips find each other.
Our tongues wrestle.
Our togas fall to the floor.

Shrugging off the responsibilities of the worlds we carry,
we find each other.

Biting

His body so new to me,
I explored it with my hands while we kissed,
and when I tired of tactile exploration,
I used my lips to touch the places my hands had traveled.
When I covered every inch of the foreign terrain of his skin
I was left still wanting.
Touch and kiss were not enough.
I wanted to consume him,
take every bit of him in.
And while I kissed his pectoral muscle,
I gave into my craving,
opened my mouth and bit down,
stopped before I broke the skin.
Feared I scared him, hurt him.
He moaned with pleasure, told me he likes it.
I felt as if I had found him,
a man who wants to be consumed
by me.

Devise and Bequeath

Steroids

He tells me about his black-market purchase,
muscles in a vial.
I try not to look disappointed
as he tells me the price and his longing.
He wants the body of an Adonis,
he wants to be someone who gets noticed.

I tell him his beauty is inside him,
that we are not loved for the perfect bicep, penis, or pectoral.

My reply falls flat at the feet
of a man who sees a boy in the mirror,
who will inject the drug once a day for six weeks.
Pumping, injecting, and raging
to match an image he feels is worthy of love.

Project

I'm going to build you
piece by piece.
I'll assemble your life.
Gather the addresses,
make a map.
Track your employers,
make a timeline.

I'll construct a picture
of what you've been doing
since we last spoke.
Graph the ups and downs of your relationships.

But most of all, I'll
be erecting a composite
of the life I haven't
been kept abreast
of—wondering
if I was ever missed.

Ex's Webpage

I fumble onto my recent ex's webpage.
A page designed to solicit sex.
I feel uneasy.
It starts off, "Hi, guys!"
and I think how he is now courting en masse.
How nothing is sacred,
that what he shared with me will be shared with all.
But I am not naïve.
There is nothing physically I could have given him
that I had not given to others.
And I think about what was between us,
how after we broke up we had sex.
The motions void of the unbridled emotions
we had once felt for one another.
He wrote that he is "not choosy"
and my ego's bruise blackens.

Tom

We met just before they became engaged.
While he talked of wedding plans
I kept thinking he should be with me.

Days before the ceremony
he told me how he felt.
Questioned if the ring on his finger was right
Questioned if he was marrying the right person.

The wedding happened, frustrations set in.
During the long talks we had at night
on the dock, on the couch, on the hood of my car
he never tried to kiss me, never made a move
that would break a vow.
His physical commitment to a contract
made me love him more.

I withdrew
to not create complications
for the newlyweds
or myself.

His e-mail arrived two years later.
By that time, 3 relationships had failed, I felt weak.
He wrote how he dreams about me, misses our talks.
He dropped by one morning, within an hour we were in bed.
I touched his sacred skin.
Kissed his lips.

It was the start of an affair
and the end of my dreams of being with him.
Not only did his marriage stand in the way.
It was his unfaithfulness.

But loneliness and weak flesh
allowed him back in my bed
as I consumed the only thing
he could now offer.

You Don't Have to Drink a Quart of Milk...

At my lips, I knew better.
Loneliness and lust
kept me sipping,
consuming what I knew
I didn't deserve.
But beliefs about myself
kept me gulping,
kept me hoping
that the bottom of the quart
would have a different taste.

Class Ring

I remember holding the catalogue.
I'd breeze past the logos for
sports and academics and kept looking for my identity:
Future Farmers of America,
French Club,
Future Business Leaders of America,
I had two blank spots to fill.
Classmates sweated over which ones to choose.
I sweated over finding at least one.
Brian Patrick ordered his early,
showed it off to me in biology class.
A diver on the left side and the school mascot on the other

I don't miss not getting the ring.
At times I miss and long for
being someone who would have fit in wearing one.
Someone who could easily decide
what image would emblazon the side.

UNIVERSAL

My friend who of physical perfection
tells me about his feelings of inadequacy
as musclemen rove the nearby dance floor.

I listen, awed by his confession,
not a desire for more
but a fear of not being enough.

Water, food, and love
are not the only universals.

In that moment
I wanted to shake him, kiss him, touch his face.
I wanted him to know
there was no reason to worry, to doubt, to be discontented.
We are all slaves to a feeling
whose rival is self-love,
whose force is the desire to be loved.
It leads us to cosmetic counters, cosmetic surgeons,
and daggers we throw at others.

It also led to a confession on the edge of a dance floor
as I realized no one is immune.

Auden's Edit[1]

I wonder why he omitted it.
The omitted line more powerful than the entire poem.
A gem published fully after his death.
It engulfs the other words, lines, stanzas.

Maybe it was expurgated to be used elsewhere
but never had.
And so we find this line,
this orphan child,
not knowing why he abolished it from its home.
Left it a strikethrough after that early draft.
Auden wrote then edited out
We must love one another or die,
a truth so sweeping
one would think there could be an exception,
a falsehood about it
but there isn't. It stands there,
in all of its opulent truth
waiting for us to realize
waiting for us to notice.
Indifference towards others is a four star general in the army of war.
And Auden, with his mightier than sword pen,
wrote how we could find salvation.
How we could escape the death and killing of war.
We must love one another or die.

---

1 After the first printing of the war poem "September First, 1939," Auden decided that it was "trash." Re-reading the line— *We must love one another or die*—he said, "Well that's a damned lie! We must die anyway." And he omitted the phrase.

Debbie May

Shortly after her arrival in the sixth grade
she was made fun of,
a pudgy girl who was the first to wear a bra
and the last to get a boy's attention.
Her name seemed to roll off of tongues
with the disdain and disgust that was
originally reserved for blacks.
Whether tenacious or needy,
she never stopped trying.

The Friday before Spring Break
she showed up in a backless floral shirt,
a shirt that would have gained compliments
had it been worn by another girl.
But not Debbie,
she was laughed at.
I knew what she felt
in that designer shirt in front of the mirror.
She thought that this was going to be it,
that this was the time they would see her beauty.
But they only saw her weakness and prayed upon it like vultures.
She sat a few desks away from me and I wondered
why she didn't give up,
didn't submit,
didn't die.
But I knew the answer
was growing inside me
and was alive inside of Debbie.

My Mother Tells Me She Wants Pajamas, Preferably Flannel

I wonder if my father ever longs for days past,
when she cared for her body.
When she adorned it at night with silk or satin,
not the middle-aged softness of flannel.
Or if her age and mass
have finally given him the wife he dreamed of;
one that cooks, spends time at home, is faithful.

Shoeboxes are filled with photos from before my birth.
Photos of their world before me,
before life was documented in albums.
Four photos stand alone in my memory,
shots of my bikini-clad mother in the house,
not sunning on the lawn,
but posing with the Zenith television behind her.
Smiling, a hand at her hip, and her body's trophy behind the camera.

I wonder if he always knew she couldn't be faithful.
If he thought he, and their vows, were not enough,
could not give her body what it wanted.
As her stomach's skin became stretched
and nursed breasts became drooped from use,
did he feel as if I would keep her from wandering?
But two men were not enough.

Reasons

It's as if her shoes fit me.
That I slid into her Candies
and lived the life she secretly led.
A ring on her finger as she'd flirt, court, and sleep with
men who were around.
I, her son, as an adult
used to do the same, sans ring.
At times I hated her for her infidelities.
The difference
wasn't just shoe size or ring
but the reasons might
have been the same.

Gaetan Dugas[2]

You couldn't have been the first
But that is how we know you.
Patient Zero, who started it all
More like Ground Zero of the disease.
Cinema and history books have marked your name as a monster.
A French bomber detonating the disease
in each ass and mouth he encountered.
But I have more faith in humans than that; I have more faith in you.
A man with only one public photo, your blond hair
swirling above your head like Einstein's.
I tracked down that photo,
wanted to see who was to blame, who was responsible
for the deaths of my friends.
And there you were,
looking like you had been captured by the shutter
while on an amusement ride.
I kept staring at you, your toxic body long departed from earth.
I kept staring and felt sadness that we've rewritten your history.
How could you have known, as a lover,
that while you wooed them with your accent and charms
while you gave pleasure, that you were also killing.
Planting poisons that they'd share with others.
I think of you standing at the front of a plane,
your steward's uniform pressed and crisp,

---

2 French-Canadian flight attendant and extensive world traveler Gaetan Dugas was labeled in 1982 as "Patient Zero" for the AIDS virus (then known as GRID, Gay Related Immune Deficiency) by the Center For Disease Control. Dugas was connected sexually to 41 of the first 248 reported cases in the country and 9 of the first 19 cases in Los Angeles. In 1980, by his own estimation, he had intercourse with 250 partners a year until his death on March 30, 1984.

You pointing with two fingers to the exits and aisle lights,
miming how to use the oxygen mask and life vest.
I like this image, you were interested in saving lives,
not killing.
You liked to serve and please.
That is what you did,
offered love wrapped in barbed wire, not knowing
and the unknowing is why
I forgive you.

Josh

Age eleven, at summer's end,
I watched my thin redheaded neighbor change
from bathing suit to Boy Scout uniform.
Watched his naked body,
marveled at the freckled pigment.
The strongest image was when
he stepped into his white underwear.
I glimpsed the barely-hidden hole of his ass.
Large, puckered, swollen—slight bruises on his hips.

After seeing gay pornography for the first time seven years later
I was able to recognize what I had seen.
His little boy's ass had been used.
Who was taking advantage of him?
His father? Brother? Boy Scout leader?
If he would have confided in me,
I wouldn't have thought such actions were odd.
After all, it was happening to me.
I thought every boy carried these secrets.

Recipe Box

He had a large stack of the memorial cards handed from funerals,
friends and lovers stolen by AIDS.
I had joked once,
that he might need a recipe box
to categorize and alphabetize the mounting stack.

He thought for a moment.
"That's not how recipe boxes are organized," he said,
"They are organized by course.
Great, now I'll have to decide who
is an entrée, dessert, or hors d'oeuvre."

So he began to shout out the names of his friends
and where he would place them

Jose – Entrée
Michael – hors d'oeuvre
Susan – hors d'oeuvre
Joey – Entrée
Jonathan – hors d'oeuvre
Alex – hors d'oeuvre
and for his last lover
Ramón – dessert

6th Date

We sat on his couch, facing each other,
backs against armrests,
feet intertwined.
He told me he wanted to teach me Spanish pronunciations,
asked me to repeat after him.

I attempted to mimic his words like a parrot to its owner,
struggled with the rolling "r's".
The foreign words spilled clumsily from my mouth.

He suggested he name off animals
and I was to guess which one.

He changed the lesson plan.
My feathers ruffled as I assumed
it was because I wasn't good.

He gave words for
cows,
penguins,
dogs, and
doves.

I was surprisingly good at assessing
and assuming translations.
But those weren't the words
I wanted to know from him.

I wanted to ask about
trust,
attraction,
the meaning of our feet touching,
and most of all, I wanted
to know our future.

Residue and Remainder

My Grandfather's Sport

Automatically I call
to tell him the news.
"Grandpa, I went bowling
and scored a 116."
He laughs,
"Good for you, grandson."

I realize how inconsequential it is,
it is not a score of one with ability.
My hand to the receiver was not second-guessed
and I dialed my way back to my childhood role,
to a young boy content on pleasing my grandfather.
He never hit me, said cross words
or made me play baseball.

I wonder if he even cared about my bowling score
or if he was happy I hadn't abandoned
the sport he taught me,
the sport of his life.
The pleasure in his voice answered my question.

I hadn't bowled in eight years
and was surprised at how much I remembered,
how easily I don't forget things,
and pleased at how automatically he and I
fell into our roles.

THE TALK

We swap stories on the phone
of "highway head"
and how to avoid swallowing.
While I kid her,
I feel shame
wash over me.
Is it normal
to have such an exchange with a sibling?
Not the locker room talk of two brothers
but of a brother and a sister
talking of technique, likes, and dislikes.

Do adults with different childhoods
talk with their siblings in a different manner?

Had the doors of sexual touch
not been forced open by the same neighbor,
if my parents had given love,
if others had not looked the other way,
maybe we would have another kind of conversation.

We've talked about these things before,
our candor doesn't falter.
In a family full of lies
this is what we have created.
We found each other in healing.

The Dead

I read his obituary.
Not only will he never
breathe, eat, or sleep,
he will never fuck.
I remember the hot tub,
his wandering hands,
and I feel honored
to have shared that with him.

I've shared sex
with so many
who are now dead,

been there to give a moment of pleasure
to a shortened life.

Knowing them in ways
their mourning mothers couldn't have known.
Knowing their bodies
not like the back of my hand or hometown
but as a quick destination I'd visit
for adventure, excitement, ejaculation.

I knew their bodies
when they had pulses,
when their heartbeats quickened
and their chests heaved
with the intensity of orgasm.

To desire them now feels odd
as the very vessel
I lusted for decomposes.

And when one of our sexual scenes
flashes through my mind during masturbation,

I appease my guilt,
remind myself
that this is a way I knew them.

An ex-lover's way
of honoring the dead
and honoring the places I touched
that cannot be touched again.

Put Your Head on My Shoulder

In the sun on the back porch
he places the infant against his body.
His broad chest developed from his delivery job.
Not in her parent's arms, she cries.
My grandfather rests her head on his collarbone,
side steps back and forth
and sings, "Put your head on my shoulder."
An unself-conscious singer with a large audience
and only one critic, her.
I witnessed this again and again,
my grandfather around infants.

When he held my nephew and sang his standard ballad
it occurred to me he must have done it to me as well.
I must have been in his arms,
body against his chest,
head in the crook of his neck.
I would like to think his singing soothed me,
that I didn't cry.
I think of him dancing and
holding my body before my parents hurt me,
him holding me at the only time I can reflect upon as innocent.
He knew me when I was unaffected and
"Whispered in my ear, baby."

My Mother's Green Thumb

When my sister found out her boyfriend cheated
she cried into my mother's arms, standing in the foyer
next to a dying hydrangea.
I watched as my sister, the strongest person I knew,
cried with uncontrollable breath and speech.
Though I felt for her,
I was also in awe that this is where she found comfort—
in my mother's embrace.

I look at my belly button these days,
amazed that at one time
my mother was the only one I knew, needed, relied upon
that her body was the gate to the world
I stepped through
years after my sister.

I had never found solace in her words, in her embrace.
I found the seeds of what was to become
my self-hatred, my self-doubt.
She was the gardener of the hyphenated "self" words,
whose critical spade invaded everything that I knew,
whose rake hashed over my foibles and faults.
I watched as my mother comforted my crying sister
and wondered about her green thumb.

Keeper

The best keeper of secrets
is the victim.
Seven years of journal writing,
no names of abusers given.
Just relations:
neighbor,
dad,
mom,
cousin,
teacher.
Does namelessness equate to blamelessness?

Keeping secrets inside my body
a bleeding stomach,
disabling head pains,
and a learning disability
that keeps me behind and apart from my class.
Santa watched.
Ganesh kept obstacles intact.
God's ears went deaf
and Atlas played paper, rock, scissors.

Society, deities, gods, and monsters sat still
while my ass bled,
spoons broke,
hands moved around where they shouldn't
and embraces lingered too long.

December 4th

Marked on my calendar,
celebrated every year.
A festivity those not close to me don't understand
or think of as an oddity.
A boasting and bragging of a sexual adventure,
it is the anniversary of when I first had sex.
Sixteen and in my mother's car.
An older guy with deep red lips, my accomplice,
who swallowed and in that moment I felt accepted.

I note the day because it is the closest thing
to a gay conception date.
There is no other marker or identifier.
Seeing Liberace in concert? My first wet dream?
It was in that moment that my life changed.
A world opened up to me and I never thought of going back.
I only thought of more,
more times, more experiences, more men
and I got it all.
I sought it out like a pirate with a treasure map.
I did it all, it felt like I did the entire city and maybe in a way, I did.

It isn't really when I became gay.
I know virgins who aren't any less gay
but it is the date of when the gates of gay sexual pleasure opened.
When I became familiar with a man's touch.

An elusive date,
similar to the stray cat we found.

We marked her birthday as the date she came to our house.
It was impossible to gauge when she was born,
all we knew was when she came home.

Our Last Name

"You know, I was thinking
I'd like to have a grandson."

My father's words do not surprise me.
He is telling me as a confidant,
he is telling me, knowing I am gay,
knowing I do not wish to have children.

His wishes rest on the shoulders of my sister.
The source of his grandfatherly pride will not have his name.
My father's name will end with me.

It is as if I passed the torch to my cousin
who will have to procreate and proliferate
the last name that wasn't shortened on Ellis Island,
that my great-grandfather named his bakery after,
that their father named his music store.
A name that even graced the cartons of frozen food,
the name of entrepreneurs and hard workers.

I can't help but see my father's wish, his confession to me,
as a sort of disappointment for who I am.
It isn't about a last name but a lifestyle.

He would never take me to a strip bar,
pat my back as we slam beers
ogling breasts and bikini bottoms.

We will not bond over woes caused by women,
the challenges of raising a family.

He missed out on opportunities
robbed by my gayness,
another reason to regret me.

Everyone Is Being Versatile but Me

I hear stories
of pitchers being catchers
and I get green.

Those beauty boys
who can thrust as well as spread.
Those guys who can butter the bread on both sides.
Those guys who know what being in a dog's position feels like.

I long to be one of those guys,
a guy who need not worry about
a potential partner's positioning.
A guy who can feel pleasure at the tip of his dick
and in the core of his ass.

Part of my desire to plow, pump, and play
is an envy of their bodily control;
relaxing, enjoying, ejaculating
are all feelings of wonder when I "give up the brown."

Many times I've felt sore, irritated, invaded
for only a little pleasure,
a poor trade off.

So I harden in my positioning
and avoid those that I envy.

The Ones Before Him

So this is how my past leaves me,
an adult
with a lover beside me in bed.

A lover I don't trust
because of the past.
Not the past with him
but my past.

Courting an Older Lover

He reminds me of the years between us
and I wonder if I'm searching for a father.
He sees our ages as a problem more than I
and I wonder if this is a symptom of my youth.

I wouldn't wish for him to trade in the experiences of his years
or make excuses for his age.
I do not see the years as obstacles but as reasons.

I promise him, I will do things
that to his older eyes will seem foolish and youthful.
I also promise him that I will resent his age
when our energy and enthusiasm are not the same.
I can also guarantee that with each other
we will grow in ways we never expected.

I wonder if his reminder isn't also to himself;
not doubting his interest in me
but doubt in the vessel
holding his feelings,
me.
He might see me with my youth as careless,
so careless to hold him with only one hand.
I do not blame him for his fears.
This is the way of youth,
to believe in the unlimited.
I want to reassure him
that my interest in him is unlimited.

Relationship Mantra to Avoid Hurt

Forever is an illusion.
Discipline your desire.

Are You Embarrassed to Be Seen with Me?

I asked the question,
a common question in the house I grew up in.
I looked to my friend for an answer,
who cringed at the question,
cringed at what lay under it,
cringed at my abandon when asking.
The unconsciousness of it all,
the lack of anything but my looks to define me.
"Would you be embarrassed to be seen with me?"
She alters her pursed mouth and smiles slightly.
The facial expression a mother would give to a foolish child,
"Steven, you never need to ask that question again."
It was the first time I questioned the question
that I had never asked to anyone else
but my parents and the mirror.

What are you going to pay for that with? Your good looks?

It was said as a reminder
to keep my desires in place.
Tongue-in-check implication was my looks weren't
enough to be of value.
That I had nothing else besides the poor quality of my face.
It was also a hint at their unwillingness to pay for things
standard in the role of a parent.

Their saying was always present,
even when they weren't.
It kept me impoverished, disempowered, wanting.

My idol in Miami
reading and signing a book I longed to hear her read from.
This was the biggest desire of my 22-year-old life,
not knowing how I'd afford gas to get there.
The mail came and I opened the envelope,
a check for my modeling underwear at a club.
I thought of my parents.
I wanted to dial the phone and answer the question.

Yes.

Italo

My ex-boyfriend's number wasn't working.
Countless calls,
empty phone lines,
I called his work.
I am told he died months earlier.
Sporadic interaction drawback,
important information is delayed.
Empty phrases complete the call,
I set the receiver down,
another AIDS casualty for statistics.
Shock is too gentle a word.

100%

My grandfather pulls me aside,
shows me his cardigan,
baits me for a compliment.
I'm hooked.
I comply.
He tells me it is wool,
opens the right side, shows me the tag
100% virgin wool.
He brings out his charming smile,
"You know how hard it is to find a virgin these days."
I laugh at his joke
and keep laughing as a reward to him
because I like that he has shared this with me.
I enjoy the role of grandson.
He is the only man who can take me there.
I fear my other relationships with men
could end what we have together.
A man
whose 78-year-old body carries him through his weekly routine:
3 games of golf, 2 games of bocce ball,
and dancing on the ballroom floor.

His comment only to me,
his humor was not lost on his 20-year-old gay grandson.
He must know.
I've never said it;
I've never not said it.
The joke—universal.
Is that why he told it?

He had told me of times in the army,
his valued possession a photo of the
green-eyed blond beauty with thin lips

who would become
his wife,
the mother of his children,
my grandmother.

He told me that when he was 13 he learned
why women were to be respected.
He saw a mare giving birth.
He stood there for hours
as blood, embryonic fluid, and water
poured out of her.
Finally a foal was born
and my grandfather was never the same.
"Stevearino, after that I never talked back to my mom, I always held the door for the ladies, I vowed to be a good husband. You see, I realized that women create miracles."

His life has been centered around women,
this is something we do not have in common.
We laughed over virgins
but thought of different ones.

My grandfather,
a man
who pats my head,
rubs my back,
kisses my cheek,
tells me he loves me,
and hopefully,
isn't ashamed that other men do the same.

Supermarket

I see him in the canned food aisle.
Before I can turn around, our carts meet.
His tall thin body the way I remember,
his dreadlocks longer,
a leather cuff on his wrist,
and a woman holding his hand.
We say hello, an introduction to his girlfriend.
We shake hands and I feel the softness of her palm,
the delicate hold of her fingers.
I'm reminded, again, the feel of a woman's touch.
This is something he knows more of lately.

I was inside him a year ago and I wonder
if he ever longs for that kind of touch.
If it is a trade-off he can manage
or if such touches by men are no longer desired.

It isn't his penchant for both that saddens me.
It isn't witnessing the team of bulk shoppers.
It isn't my cart of single servings.
I feel a longing, not for the thin dreadlocked man
or the woman with soft hands.
But I long for feeling comfort in such hands,
long for a desire to want women,
to be seen as normal.

Immediately I am ashamed of my desire,
feeling like a traitor to my community.
But I know the grass is greener.

I remember when my feet were on that grass,
the greenery as abundant as the praise
of how my looks would get the ladies.

It seems easier for those
who desire what is accepted,
who love what is approved.

But I know who I am.
I know that holding the hand of a woman
would not ease feelings of loneliness,
it would only add to them.

She Knew

In a dream
I'm with my neighbor.
We are boys standing in the basement of my boyhood home.
He is holding me down, touching me and I
become aware there is someone watching.
My mother is there.
The touching continues, but my fear is replaced with shame.
My mother does nothing except watch.
I feel her anger, her disgust, her disappointment.
It is directed at me.

I wake up from the dream.
I can't cry.
I write it down to prevent amnesia,
She knew.

I shouldn't have been surprised when I heard
about mom not confronting her brother
when my sister complained
of a cousin who fondled, felt-up, and fingered
places of her anatomy she couldn't even name.

By not telling my mother,
I was spared the knowledge she wouldn't have done anything.
Spared 20 years of having this unnamed feeling.
In a way my silence did protect me.
Until the dream and penned note beside my bed.

Pottery Class

His fingers interlace with mine.
My heart beat seems louder,
then I remind myself
that this is a lesson,
not love or affection,
as a straight man guides my hands on the spinning clay.
My thin fingers had almost forgotten the potency of touch,
the exchange of energy.
All of this eludes him as he attempts to show me
how to balance a piece of earth.
He tells me to close my eyes,
feel the clay, not just see it.
The class had already disappeared
as his experienced hands eclipsed mine on the clay.
I fight the urge to stop
this act that my body translates as intimacy.
Not only is he a married heterosexual
but I'm sure another's touch is not foreign to his hands.

His touch doesn't seep into the sectors
of my heart reserved for lovers,
it moves into the vacant room reserved for my father's love,
a man who hadn't loved me long before I told him I was gay.

My teacher pushes my hands
into the earth that soon becomes balanced.

I wish my father's touch would have come
with as few strings and as much encouragement.

Together we center clay.
Separately, I awaken to touch again,
learn a craft, and choose my father.

Mother

My bookshelves are lined with women
who speak out in the moments
you had been silent.

Some of their words lack luster
but jacket photos show them to possess
a style, dare I say beauty,
you never had.

As for my favorite writer
the diarist
she possessed the sympathy you lacked.

The bold black poet
gave me less to fear,
gave me comfort.

Reviewing my bookshelf I appear
more like a lost boy than bibliophile.

Seeking out a mother figure
from women who mother words.

I seek out women who cared for what they created,
who took time to polish, craft, and caress
what was once inside them
that will now wander the world.

5th Grade Photo

I notice it in its oval frame on his end table,
comment to my grandfather
"I can't believe you still have this photo."
He reminds me that I've commented on it before.
Less than a year after it was taken, I begged him to hide it.
I'd always hated that photo of me.
Hair parted and feathered,
fat features, big cheeks, big nose.
The photo of an unattractive awkward boy who didn't know
that pain could end.

I hold the oval photo, think of myself in the 5th grade.
He finally offers, after 17 years, to remove it.
Says that if I'm still bothered by it, that he would get rid of it.
In that moment I feel deep love
as he offers to respect my wishes from adolescence.

I tell him that he can keep it out.
I like that he held his ground firmly for so long
and silently wonder what he likes about the image,
what he loved about the boy in the photo.
I place it back onto the table, look at the boy
and wonder when I might love him as well.

About the Author

Steven Reigns is a Los Angeles-based poet and educator. After earning a degree in Creative Writing at the University of South Florida, he published his début poetry collection, *Your Dead Body is My Welcome Mat*, in 2001. Since then, Reigns has published four chapbooks: *Ignited*, *Cartography*, *In the Room*, and *As if Memories Were Not Enough*. A two-time recipient of The Los Angeles County's Department of Cultural Affairs' Artist in Residency Grant, Reigns organized and taught the first-ever autobiographical poetry workshop for GLBT seniors and edited an anthology of their writings, *My Life is Poetry*. He has taught writing workshop around the country to GLBT youth and people living with HIV and recently received his Masters in Clinical Psychology from Antioch University. Currently he is involved with *S(t)even Years*, a 7-year endurance performance under the mentorship of performance artist Linda Montano.

www.StevenReigns.com

About the Publisher

The mission of Sibling Rivalry Press is to develop, publish, and promote outlaw artistic talent—those projects which inspire people to read, challenge, and ponder the complexities of life in dark rooms, under blankets by cell-phone illumination, in the backseats of cars, and on spring-day park benches next to people reading Plath, Ginsberg, and Whitman. We welcome manuscripts which push boundaries, sing sweetly, or inspire us to perform karaoke in drag. Not much makes us flinch.

For more information, visit us online.

www.SiblingRivalryPress.com

CPSIA information can be obtained at www.ICGtesting.com
Printed in the USA
LVOW132348130113

315480LV00002B/680/P